STORY LINE PRESS POETRY SERIES

Backtracking / Vern Rutsala / 1985

The Double Genesis / Dennis Sampson / 1985

The Reaper, Inc.
Santa Cruz, California

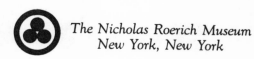

The Nicholas Roerich Museum
New York, New York

BACKTRACKING

Vern Rutsala

Story Line Press
Santa Cruz, California
1985

ACKNOWLEDGEMENTS

Portions of this book have appeared in *Poetry Now, Portland Review,* and *The Reaper.*

I want to thank the National Endowment for the Arts for a fellowship which was of great help during the writing of this book.

Special thanks should also be given the Guggenheim Foundation for a fellowship which allowed me to bring *Backtracking* to its final form.

ISBN 0-934257-00-0 (paperback)
ISBN 0-934257-01-9

First Printing, 1985

Printed in the United States of America.

Published by Story Line Press, a subsidiary of The Reaper, Inc., 325 Ocean View Avenue, Santa Cruz, California 95062. All rights reserved.

Book design by L. Howard-McDowell

To Joan

Contents

Out there, where frontiers end, roads are erased.

Octavio Paz

The table is round

And so is my memory
*   *   *
It will never end
This dream of crystal

Pierre Reverdy

Experience Idaho
A WORLD OF FUN

I discover the road as I go forward,
And curse the faintness of sunset and dawn.

T'ao Ch'ien

The whisper of the wind in
            that pine-tree . . .
is sweet as the murmur of live water

William Carlos Williams
from "Theocritus: Idyl I"

The Lake

1.

The morning paper hits the porch
and all my vocabulary fades,
headlines steal every word
leaving nothing but bone.
So I play possum until evening
dreaming the ancient monster's
form dripping algae and dead
time — my words gone, the air
used up and still.
                    But when
the paper goes to bed I sweep up
syllables like a janitor until
I have them all again except
the twenty-five I leave
my disc jockeys. I even
trespass on my neighbors' words,
ready to use their bleak
utensils — their "huh's" and "I
told you so's," their grunts
and wheezes. I keep after them
all, especially the never-to-be-
spoken they grind to powder
with their teeth in sleep.

And because I can I call
the street a lake, black ice rippling,
the old algae shuffling in.

2.

Past midnight the sun rises and I
walk old ties by the mill, taking
up that stuttering gait, eating
a Jubilee candy bar. The lake's blue
bubble glistens on my left. On my
right the glinting foil of silver
storage tanks.
                  Here I let the monster
rise breaking the blue glisten
of the lake,
              rise snorting and curling
like a Chinese dragon.

                All water
has its monster, that surge of rumor,
that need curdling depths
                  and one summer
we found ours
            and with him
the little glory
          we could stand.

3.

The summer people never saw us
no matter where we stood. We

were audience, clammed-up witnesses,
big eyes for their boats and cars.
Somehow they owned us, allowed us
to spend our bitter winters
with their summer cabins.

                                    Before our
monster came the town was
half-asleep, dreaming through dinners,
living one day like another —
a wide place in the road.

                                    But then
we bloomed for one whole season,
the yellow glow of fame fanning
down from the lookout —
a monster made us human.

4.

All that summer we went out
in Bob's blue rowboat every chance
we got. Each deadhead grinned
like our cherished monster, the great
slimy pet we would be the first
to see. He was our own murky
creature and he dredged us up
from all our anonymous gloom
until the drugstore couldn't stock
enough copies of the Sunday supplement
that put us on the map.

5.

But, no matter what I do tonight,
the lake freezes over and the summer
cabins are too far away to vandalize
or burn
            and I pull back, waiting
for the morning paper's signal,
invention running down, rubbed raw
by nights like this, the old piston
crystalized, held together with glue.

What I want is all that oblong
past —
            an old summer reeling in
drunk and disorderly,
                        the summer
people and the long long legs
of their untouchable daughters,
teeth like mints, eyes like .22s,
that lake, that monster basking
and winking and nodding.
But the lake is frozen and lost —
the monster locked up for good.

II

Nightwalk

Slumped houses, rain, struggling
branches of winter trees —
I disappear
between the streetlights, entering
old places, half-life
shadows, toothpicks of memory,
ready for travel,
talked into it by chill, wet
streets, the witless coma
of blank windows, ready
to spend my time
on the washboard past the pond,
past the heartless shacks
where the skeletons lived.
Caught in the dance
I move fast
by the thicket near the tracks
where hobos jungled-up
in summer, past the mill,
haystack burner glowing
sparks to the sky, travelling
hard, skimming
a new path — that one
crawling under weeds,
inching home on its
drunken knees, leading to
the vacant lot, the place
of broken hopes and rust.
This is better, streetlights

the night's dinner, houses
thundered back to lumber.
I have to push beyond
hobo jungles, beyond the dump,
the fractured cars, the bald
tires of spent passion.
I have my instructions now —
disappear and they're
clear, let the street dissolve
and the aim is simple.
I must police up the past,
pick up all
the intimate losses
in my paper suitcase,
look all night
for discards and empties
and find at last
the exact place
we buried our riches,
the coffee can of old sorrow.

III

The Empty House

Again I answer the cold phone, again
I hold my breath between each
word, again I fly
                    over snow-dusted plains.
I give up each possession. I turn off
the last light. Like a hobo I travel.
(Nameless, all the lights go out.)
A bat weaves an arc like an eyelash
on the sky and all the roads
roll up. When I sleep I sleep
under bridges. When I sleep

I dream this dream.
                    Candles
in the windows die.
A scarecrow clucks his tongue.
Dead weeds beside a road draw out
a longing for the stark, the barren,
the faded lives of sticks and rocks,
husks, frozen seeds —
                    and the windows
die as well.
                    No streetlight burns.
I grope my dark way back
tasting asphalt and gravel.
Road oil films my eyes.
All the lights go out.
                    I follow signs —
blinkers, arrows, any hint.

Metal clinks in alleys.
Shapes flap like maimed dogs.
And again it's there
                    the house
a ruin
        a shack lost in the woods,
only leaves and dust breathing softly.

Then it all twists off the page
with Thalidomide and despair.
It's been another night
of coaxing and refusal and I'm
like a mover carrying vacancy
into those rooms, a trip for each
spoon, one cup of emptiness
at a time, a single word
in each hand:
                    Nothing.

Nameless
        all the lights go out,
all the roads roll up,
candles in the windows die
and the windows die as well —
house and town, the dim
ways we came
                    dissolve.

It is late. We must invent

those backtrack routes —
                              without words
we lose the way — invent
every step we came, invent
words for every grand
crackpot model of our lives
built in garages and bottles.

Somehow with these words I've
got to build my own boat
in the cellar, find my visionary
chicken ranch of ease, my
beefsteak mine, my leather orchard.

I want the old swamp, the dogs
that died, sentiment smelted down
to an ore that counts
                              in the meadows
of déjà vu
              and deeper still.
A winter night
              provides the fuel.

IV

What We Looked For

We wanted the strange,
needed to own
that strangeness
we knew was there
in the cold lake bottom,
in the deep woods
and our dreams.
There were times Bob
hid in the woodshed's
rafters and brought
that whole cold shed
alive with his horror
movie laugh, making
the stacked wood
and axe speak
the agony of wood
and steel, scaring
himself down
into a Wolfman
crouch, giving the dark
a name we couldn't speak.
What we wanted was
always there in the cellar,
the lake, and the huge
demon barn of the woods.
It was the fever you
caught at night deeper
than fevers wood ticks
gave, a fever brought

by the bear and the giant
bat, the great owl
of the dark,
and at its center
no monster, only
the night like a drain
of black water swirling
you down forever
toward its ancient
quicksand heart.

V

The Tree

1.

My neighbor's crippled tree
speaks in the icy air,
an amputee climbing toward
light, its huge trunk bald,

lopped limbs helpless, but
the few live branches still
climb the cobweb ladder
toward the sun.

The tree hangs on, sending
its litany out and away,
seeking connection the way
these lines seek exits

through fissures in the dark.

Sick tree, I climb your limbs
every night. I pick your
apples and acorns, I pick

your sweet peaches. You're
my partner in this game
of travel back and in.

They beat hell out of you,

choke your sap, jam your

arteries but you hang on
determined to present
your few chewed leaves

when winter finally lets
your bad circulation go
and you speak the true story
of these battered houses.

2.

But today they cut the tree
down. Last night I didn't know
my words could bring the saw
so soon. Now it looks makeshift,

an imitation, a battlefield tree,
half itself already stacked
at its own foot.
                    It tells me

to stop. That exits are healing
over, roads sinking so far away
no junked car could ever
find them.

                    Those ruts that fit
my tires like fingerprints

are silt tonight and the city
has finally built a wall

so thick
          not even my sharpened
spoon
          can tunnel out.

3.

I feel miles piling up inside.
I feel aches and blisters
forming.
          I look at the lopped tree,

all its juice gone home,
the city's comment on spring,
its old drama draining
and my ink drying too.

Now all things seem like
words heard in other rooms,
the scented breath of undertakers,
the oily tongues of salesmen.

The tree is gone. Soon enough
we'll forget how it looked,
maimed but still trying, still
flying those chewed flags in spring.

We grow restless and head out
painting our headlights across
the bony land, always looking
for the right road, that subversive path
growling in the underbrush, that
wild route, the only one
that takes us
              where time stops.
All our fury seeks that rest —
my fury running down the page,
yours curled with you. We both seek
that globed poem in the valley,
that meadow music of trees
and shadows,
              our only story
is the quest. We want to hold
the ancient stick again, want
color and motion in dead
trees. And if we remember
right they come back
and the crazy lake ignites
with dead summers. We taste
water mixed with bark
and hear the mill sending
everyone home for lunch.
I meet Slim dead drunk
on Main Street and once more
take the slippery dime he offers
and then it's gone

through my fingers, Slim
dead for thirty years.
                    We have half
of correspondence, the other half
gone down the old well
that stole the moon.
                    But you taste
that water still, still
savor the flavor of icy
metal and the galvanized
lip of the dipper.
                    The hidden
tongue remembers.

VII

Part of the Story

1.

In Idaho it all ground down,
the lake seemed always
frozen. For heat
you chopped wood.
Sometimes a chip
flew in your eye. Then
you were simply a man
with one eye. Out hunting
if your best friend
shot the other one out
you were blind.
               But toughness
was honored, some irreducible
the Depression couldn't steal.
You gave up a tooth here,
a black eye there but never
gave up the final thing.
               To honor
this strangeness they set up
speakers at the lumberyard
and everyone drove over
for the second Louis-Schmeling
fight. Men sat on runningboards
and fenders passing a pint
around. Kids played in the sawdust
knowing enough to keep quiet
at something this important.

The whole town was there,
everyone in that ring, quivering
in the static.

　　　　We measured history
with fights: How Harvey knocked
that cheating doctor on his ass,
how the Roland boys took on
the whole town of New Meadows.
You tasted blood early, the flavor
like tears while your father
watched, his silence saying times
were tough, trouble resolved
itself hard. If you were wrong
you suffered. If you were wrong
you lost a few of vanity's rotten
teeth. If you were right you still
laid off a few days, flicking
your tongue in the gaps.

　　　　And so
we all drove over for Louis
and Conn but we don't go there
anymore. You can't let them
walk over you

　　　　but they do.

2.

Something was coming, some giant

bulldozer, some heavy equipment
nightmare bringing change.
                                Feeling
this rumble in their nerves
some fought or drank, some
got religion, the only allegiance
available, jumping in that church
like a lake, their old thirst
making them holler, talk in tongues,
wrinkle the hell out of their Sunday
best and get down on their knees
to lick their tongues dry on that
slivery floor and wind up
begging Jesus for just one more
drink in paradise.
                          Mainly people
found hard pleasures where
they could, feeling the earth shudder,
changing partners at a dance
and never bothering with the paperwork.

But something was coming, some
March of Time voice about to announce
the end of it all for Holy Roller
and drunk. There was a hidden
frenzy
            and the giant growl of diesel
in the next valley,
                          earth movers throbbing.

It was then the hard coil within
broke up and some Elsewhere loomed
demanding allegiance,
                    and we felt
our legends sink away
                    and drift slowly
to the lake's bottom
                    where the sad
carcass of our monster lay,
                    great
cathedral ribs
            empty forever.

VIII

The sky is clear for February's false
spring, moonlight icing leafless trees
and dreamless houses.
                    I walk my
neighborhood counting dark windows,
sensing the locks' clenched teeth.
Each house looks abandoned,
dreamers stolen, and all the streets
are mine. I travel this illusion
and long for a single light, even
some forty watt sign of life, some
unknown companion struggling
with his income tax or even reading.
Of course I find none.
                    And most days
my neighbors lock me in, hard
stares like shoulders on the door
though we have mastered the art
of the wave, one arm telling whole
histories two or three times
a month.
                    Some evenings Fixit's
power tools grit my teeth for hours.
Heloise and Abélard next door —
when we first met he offered drinks,
a fine beginning but it's been all
downhill since. Now she averts
her eyes as if following doctor's
orders though I always speak

enjoying the quick slew of her
baby blues.
                    Good Samaritan collects
for funeral wreaths and always has
a card to sign big as a menu.
But there are
                    the faceless ones I like —
window shades and empty cars
their only language, saying no one
is here. They spread out and out
silently, covering miles, neighborhoods
rising and falling, dreamers struggling
and the night thick with visions
and cries and the routes I want
to take.
                    Now and then a word
lights up, a line flexes and my
thin artery to the lost place
flashes a signal
                    but then the sleeping
houses lock me in, tie my tongue
and teach me the virtues
of wordlessness. The widow's
stare from her window steals
my keys and tires, clots my
ink and the old road blocks
are up. The imagination ordinance
is broken at your own risk.
It's this street's sure felony.

                                        Even
my pen says no, the paper
refuses my tickets so I back
and fill
            travelling the sleeping
houses,
            wanting to crack them
like oysters
                and find their secrets.
And so I break
                    and enter house
after house, wander the dim rooms,
trying to tell them apart. Each
is too familiar, each mirrors
each.

        To think we came all that
way, risked everything, used our
bodies for plows and arrived here
with these lives of dim sensation —
clock-tick
            floor-creak
                        furnace-knock.

IX

Crystal

In this winter stutter and lack
of spark, this growl of starters
in the snow grinding hard, I
give back all the words
and wonder only if the old snowcrust
in the meadow will still support
me. Can I go crosscountry
with eyelashes of frost, nostrils
freezing and thawing with each
breath? I remember the meadow,
its winter metamorphosis,
but a blizzard rises here.
I go in circles, tethered to some
strange center telling me
to sleep, some spinning funnel
drawing me down. And I do
sleep, my hobo dreams fall
to crystal breaking, wine bottles
shatter on and on falling
and falling toward some pure
crystal center and in this dream
I know that we all twist
toward that vacancy, that heart
of glass, that bony crystal,
that spirit of resurrected empties,
that home of irreparable damage.
But now deep inside the dream
I find the frozen town.
A white wind creases the air,

the snow like broken glass,
and every familiar house
is vacant, roofs caved in,
walls askew, wind blasting
that vacancy. Everyone gone!
A furious ghost town frozen
in place. I can't believe it —
to have come this far to this! —
and like an insane mailman
I seek out each one
and tick it off — *Gone, Gone,
Gone.* Winter and time have
killed each one. No blowtorch
dream can set this right.
Then I hear the crystal break
again, I hear every gritty
bit. I lose, tonight I lose
and to get back I must·
invent a new alphabet
to make this world live, to keep
it from this sleep of ice.
New alphabet, new language,
new vocabulary of heat —
a language hot enough to melt
that crystal back to sand.
Hot enough to thaw
the frozen lake, hot enough
to breathe the dead back
from blast and nothingness,
hot enough to swell and build
until walls and roofs return
and all the lights go on.

X

The Parked Car

V.M.R. 1916-1961

It's the steady quest
                    compass spinning
No direction
            but the pulse
Of obsession
            beginning and ending
In this room
            as rain falls
No direction
            but the swirling intestine
Quest
        for the old labyrinth
                        The place
We carry gleaming
                like a golden
Vertebra
        like the shining coin
In reflection pools
                that finally winks
a beer can's
            dark triangle eye

Identity stretches far
                    a dim pulse
Travelling dead wires
                    from this room
In that reach to nurture
                        dead time

With the only tools
                    at hand
                              words
Tracking down the page

Now I hear the hum of tires
As I travel back
                    counting each RPM
All the way
                    to a parked car's
Stillness
          with a woman sitting there
Through long
              gray afternoons
Day after day
                And I'll never know
How far that still
                    car travelled
As she sat alone
                  at twenty-six
Dreaming her long thoughts

We move from wilderness
To wilderness
                A parked car in '42
This crosshatched winter
                              light
This swirled oak table
                        I read

With my fingers
                And the rain tonight
Becomes that rain
                and my street
Becomes her street
                but the years
Will not collapse
                I'll never know
Where she travelled
                or how far
Or why
                The only way out
Of this wilderness of time
Is invention
                The only way to cheat
This hunger is to fix
                that car
Beside the curb
                with the young woman
Sitting through the afternoon
Day after day
                as you might sit
Dreaming a city
                into being
Around you
                This first and last
City of your life

Long Distance ——————————————

1.

All night I seek an easement, effort
socked-in, impulse grounded. All
night I petition hard, hammering
the city hall of my neighbors' dreams.
The only way out is against the law,
something you always knew.

To get beyond the snares you
have to move like a poacher, like
an outlaw road builder, a pirate highwayman
who paves his own way, ignoring
all signs, veering away from all the rules.
Thus my way is by disguise,

                        underbrush
scarcely touched by my single lane,
my gravel path.
             I chew the rock myself
spitting out the six-inch road,
                    adding

my teeth, anything.
             I must get there
again and again, get there and poach
on the past
         bloodlessly.
This is the poem's

dream. The poem is hungry
for the dream of resurrection, the failing
dream grown strong with the muscles
of helplessness, with the ink of the invisible.
Which is why I write my way back
with gravel, inventing my own Watts Tower

of death and viscera
                    my DNA model
twisting more obscure
                        than backroads
travelled only once
                    by drunks.

2.

The present is all transition,
all joint and intersection.
Nothing happens
but the synapse jump
of fear, the outside agitator
swallowed whole, each man his own
agent against himself, calling it perhaps
the city hall
of his neighbors' dreams.
Perhaps.

But this is why I

saddle up each night
and write these old roads down,
these arteries of memory
through the accident of grit and need —
the avenue of words
pulsing hard
toward invention
as if the first act
of calling long distance
were to invent the telephone
and then the person being called.

XII

What You Do

You explore old places
for no reason.

They call. You go,
uncovering shadow and dust,

tasting history in bits.
The texture of a screen

opens dead summers. You recall
the lake, the meadow, the hill

and the flavor of dirt
by the depot where the snow

melted first. This is history,
your own dim access.

You remember the intimate —
old toys, the smell

of bark and water, the slap
of waves on the boat dock,

hot gravel on your feet.
The motion is back

from present trouble, this swarm
of flies, back

to that first memory
like a light snapped on

when you found yourself
alone and distance yawned

the first chasm. Later, grayness
crumbled around you, the sky

falling, the world dropping away
from the car window,

the woodshed's darkness
suddenly fierce

with the animals risen
from your pillow . . .

XIII

Upstairs just now I stood
in the hall letting the rafters
settle on my shoulders,
listening to the sleepers,
and then fell down this page
again —
            the only snow in town.
And the mood of elegy
falls, my words soaking in it
like rags. It forms as my
neighbors do a roadblock,
the mound of grief between
Here and There.
            The mood
of elegy falls, dusting meetings
with old friends. We talk
and smile, uncover gems
of anecdote, polish the stones
of memory from a past neat
as a display case, that
museum we visit.
            But I feel
myself listening, always
listening for some other voice,
some other past.
            What I hear
is like a cough at night
from an upstairs room,
some old message I never
understood, and wherever I am

I listen for such sounds —
night cries from a child
never born. I lurch toward
him, trying to capture the cause
of nightmare, the dark
comment of a cough.
                    It's for
this poem I listen, this poem
and the huge wilderness
it moves toward — the way
the woods closed darkly
behind the old house, the way
the dark breathed hard
at apartment doors.
                    I stand
in the hall again and feel
the yokes of the rafters settle.
I keep the house together
through this deep winter,
but for pay I want a long ride
by Greyhound and then travois.
The long hard ride
until I reach that other
winter and high country,
until I pass the timberline
where the world becomes
rock and ice — a place
higher than any we have known,
higher than rafters and pages,
higher than every destination.

The Guest

When the house is full of people,
the fire snapping, I find myself
looking out toward the dark street,
staring into its icy silence expecting
someone else, expecting the person
who never comes.
                    I sense him
waiting outside, a shadow under
a tree, a slumped figure
in an abandoned car — the great hobo
Wobbly ghost of everything
                              waiting there
                                        warmed
by our lights, listening to our sounds.
But then the party's current pulls me back
and I forget.
                    Yet now with everyone asleep
I write this letter to him, this
endless letter night after night, hoping
perhaps to catch him at some whistle stop
before he hops a freight or around some
dim fire, straining sterno through
cotton gauze.
                    I feel he was outside just now
in a beat-up pickup
                    and all that's left
of whatever compelled us across continents
and gave us arms enough to clear land
and farm rocks for nourishment.

Gray ghost
beyond streetlights, fugitive from neighborhoods
like this, the only one who knows
the accurate way to travel — follow the sun,
follow crops — but he fades like
a migratory bird, like mosquitoes
in the first chill.

XV

My Buddies

My buddies breathe dust
Where the rubber plants die
The lobby of the Lotus Hotel
Rooms $5 and up
                    You can see them there
Any time
            our mirror shadows

But tonight is special
                    This is their club
The hub that draws them on rainy
Nights like this
                The murky light suits them
The dry ferns
                The streaked glass suit them

First of course is the social hour
And for those without muscatel or tokay
There's a coke machine that works
Sometimes
Later
        chili dogs and beer for the faithful

A talcum of dust rises
From the hairless sofa
                        and every chair
Sinks low as a bucket seat
"Drive to your heart's content
There ain't no speed limit here"

The chairman says
                    beaming
Everyone likes him
They voted for his thin hair
And the little broken veins
Around his nose
                    A man like that
Is honest

They gab and sulk
                    each member
Bringing out his past
                    like a snapshot
"I could've made a go
But the location was lousy"
"That woman took every fuckin cent I had"
"He cheated me blind"
"Sonofabitch"

They like this but as the wine goes round
They grow feisty
                    grinning and nodding
As they talk of heroes
                    Ex-pugs rocking
On their heels
                    The runner-up
The hot rookie who
                    the chairman says
"Succumbed to the sophomore jinx

They curved him to death"
Someone yells "Winners never quit
And quitters never win"
Everyone roars
                    "Shee-it" the chairman whoops
Dancing a jig and hooting
And now they know everyone is there
They love the list
                    sweeter than any menu
Contenders with glass jaws
                              patsies
Masters of the bonehead play
Wrong-way Roy
                    Bums-a-month
Sluggers buried in the minors
Men over the hill
                    and out of gas
Pitchers who lost it
                    All the tragic flaws
Doctor Strangeglove
The strike-out king
                    oh yes especially
The strike-out king
This is the losers' caucus
"But come on down" they yell
"We ain't particular
There's plenty a room for you"

XVI

The New Stove

The old one, ungainly, out of place
    sits by the back door, sides
streaked with old meals, buttons
    carrying old fingerprints
away — tomorrow to Union Gospel.

It was my mother's stove, our
    companion for fourteen years,
collaborator on how many meals?
    Burners black and still, oven
going cold in the weather, dead clock

deader still. Once it was her
    new stove, hers for a year
before her death at forty-five —
    clearly not good enough to keep
her alive, but good enough to

carry me this far, to forty-six
    in this kitchen where I sit
dreaming back and forth, consulting
    that dead clock and those
dark burners with no news of food —

only memories going back to a day
    in winter when the stove, unnoticed,
became ours. I remember the last
    drive to the hospital, my father
driving, my arm over the seat

to hold her hand, holding as if pulling
    her along, holding as if keeping her
from falling some great distance —
    towing that dry hand all the way.
I remember how my arm went

numb, how I wanted it to sleep
    and hurt, to somehow pay and buy
her back with stupid pain. There was
    her dry hand and her eyes
and that drive going on and on

yet too short. And there was that truck
    of junk leading us — old refrigerators,
old stoves, battered and rusty — which
    I tried to stare away but it
continued, bearing its trite symbols

of the obsolete, our culture's silly
    signs of death, and all the while
her new stove waited at home,
    shiny, guaranteed for years
and years to come . . .

XVII

The Dwelling of the Past

This poem believes in the work
ethic, believes you fashion
your own route through memory
and wilderness, blazing low
trails that dissolve overnight,
the wilderness rebuilding itself
on footprints and the bones
of travellers.
        But for guide
we have only the horseshoe bends
of pages — to the bottom and then
the perilous turn to the next,
adding lines, scattering the inky
gravel, the road fading behind us,
losing its way without our will
tamping it in place between
the shoulders.
        That gravel is these
broken syllables, the last we have
of words, their residue, the squawks
and grunts, their rock-language
baby talk.
        Yet with them we build
the dwelling of the past, word
by word, our flashcard house rising
like a tower in spite of winter
wind, in spite of darkness.
Without these words night will
enter bringing all its casualties.

Tonight they hang back and all
things meet now on the round table
mixing like the grain of oak.
But the early light dims
                    goes dirty
toward darkness, a murk descending
the water muddy where I dredge.
And now I find only the rubber
boots of cliché, the dump
                    of stereotype.
They swarm our countryside, fleeing
from the burning hills of my
neighbors' dreams.
                    But this poem believes
in the work ethic. I want
the crackpot plan, my perpetual motion
machine in a bottle, my yacht
in the cellar. I'm sick
                    of the medieval
walls of junk our cities grow,
sick of how we're forced to tug our
forelocks until we're bald, sick
of how our masters permit some
pleasure now and then, some bread —
a fleabag circus under the banner:
Never Give a Sucker an Even Break.
Which is why I travel toward my
private beefsteak mine, my
shadow home of memory. I have
the shares, I own fifty-one percent.

XVIII

The dream searches its own pockets seeking
what feeds it well, struggling or flowing
it moves across mountains, navigates
dry riverbeds, moving with its own will
wordlessly toward its nourishment —
skunk cabbage and the swamp behind
the old house, winter melted to tea.
                                    It wants
origin and seed and plows toward
its old constituency, its gods of rubber
and tin, assuming like water its own
level.
        And as it moves words follow
in wagons, in caravans. They follow
the dream's footprint blaze, uncovering
the old right of way, that smothered trail
where words must go.
                        The dream dances
and juggles. Darts like a radio signal.
Conjures dead life from nothingness and grit.
Dream finds its ways and means,
winding up all its loose ends, tracing
arteries and veins in the body electric.

But tonight and any night the riverbed
is all words have and they travel
that trough east, willing water into it,
inventing water from stone, tracking
the dream's path.

At first there's only
a dampness, then a trickle writing its
crooked penmanship in the dust, then
a stream and finally the only river
for this canoe of words.
                    We ride it hard
forcing white water from the calmest
stretch, giving nightmares to that surface.
Passion rumbles boulders through the gorge.
Huge polysyllables of rock boom and rattle
gravel. Periods and commas skitter along
the bottom and mounted fish come back
to life.
            The dream hems and haws,
coughs, clears its throat and longs for
the town beyond these dark streets
married to sleep and cold.
                            The dream longs
for green, for sun, for some deep thaw
that warms the icy kinks from our bones.
The dream crimps and twists, turning like
an old sheep trail doubling back, echoing
this table's grain, this swirl and sweep, this
deep writing beyond the legible.
                                Oh how we
egg our memories on, egg them back to
sources within a dream, some pool, some thick
liquid darkness, the swamp where everything
began — the swamp behind the old lost
house.

I work that liquid with my hands
feeling its ropes of current, its motion
like earth-shift, like birth saying Yes,
saying No.
                    But now the dream slips the hook,
abstractions take no bait and disappear
in the Oregon night of steelhead dreams,
ghost salmon, soluble trout
                              in the invented river
of words.
                    And again I balance my dear sleepers
like a juggler, thinking their rooms to
the second floor by levitation, by will
and ink.
                    Foraging the enamel night I wander
to the window, reread a friend's letter, check
a date — all fillers, all acts for the end
of the page — and the night gapes frosty
and clear, ice feeding on the roofs of cars,
the neighborhood seeming to thicken as it draws
closer in the cold, smothering my province,
my vacant house before dawn.
                              Somewhere the old
lake trembles, a brilliant sun-glitter on its
waves
          and far off, its leash broken, the dream
skirts the old fringe of town, nosing and searching,
stopped short by each familiar — each rock

and tree a close friend. One and one and one,
burgeoning toward avalanche, swelling with the ancient
dead, burgeoning, every impulse sprouting, each
signature of each thing booming and rattling
like gravel from a truck peppering down, everything
finally coming in with a crazy shotgun blast
and the dream at last cries its ecstatic uncle!

XIX

1.

I need a new car every night
and each one must be
vintage '33 or 4, scavenged from
Alaska Junk just before
the giant crusher makes them
bite size.
        I sneak in and make those
old buggies talk, sorting nuts
and bolts, scouring the city
for parts.
        The extravagance of my
poverty knows no bounds.

2.

The best night I found nearly
all the parts of the '34 we
drove to Coos Bay after Pearl
Harbor. I dredged it out
and got all the way to ice
and Idaho, past New Meadows
and nearly to the farm
before its tinfoil body crumpled.
Good American something in me
died when my resurrected roadster
quit. I felt that inner crumbling,

radiator hose
             and aorta
the same flesh.

3.

But I find others,
             hotwiring Hudsons
up on blocks for twenty years
and they work.
             On blocks they
gallop and canter
             going faster
and faster
             until they hit the good
lost road.
Studebaker Reo Model B —
all gathered in the darkness,
all waiting for some greasy-
fingered judgment day.

4.

And so hunting nuts and bolts,
scavenging the body shops, plucking
the rust-ridden from the crusher,
I find suitable transportation —
the kind I like. And most
of them use cartridge ink, ink
fuels the headlights too, headlights

drawing the map I follow.
And they can change at will,
becoming boats or kites, even
submarines. It makes no difference.
The avenue is words — we're
conveyed by the streetcar of words,
the sea-going tram of syntax.

5.

Now I travel the creases in
the map,
the folds much more
convincing than those squiggle
roads.
      I pour down a fold
arriving where it meets another
fold,
then veer off toward
the center —
              that secret interior
of maps
       where all travellers
converge.

6.

But the place is like a grease
trap and I head back
to Alaska Junk seeking

the instructions of rust,
the bland hints of dissolution.
I wander foothills of junk,
their icy shadows falling.
Something must turn up
and then, yes, I spot my ace —
the old Galloping Goose linked
with the local interurban
way down at the bottom
of the deck. Even from under
those tons I snake it out easily.

7.

Soon we're travelling hard,
grinding through wheatfields,
skidding and bouncing across
mountains, making our own
secret tracks, bell clanging
like hell. We barrel the whole
way full throttle, the Goose
finding rails anywhere it
looks, its little wheels sculpting
them from sand and rock,
the bell going crazy the whole
way announcing
                    We're Here!
We're Here!

XX

Nickel and Dimed

for Joan

Tonight we have the steady meter of the furnace
and the cold clear night rising forever
above the house. We have the dog lying in his pool
of quiet, we have our books and breathing —
the filaments weaving back and forth between us
as we read the evening up, read on and on
forever in these moments. Our street is stock-still
and the universe held between thumb and finger
like a nickel.
             But we're travellers even now
as the house churns our landscape flat as a coin.
Indian heads and buffalo dot our plains, all the coins
that bought this evening so long ago:
                      Tips for errands,
dimes for movies, even the grand clanking silver
for hamburgers and shakes, all the coins that have
passed through our fingers without a trace.
                   Moving now,
while we sit stock-still, the house seems to mint
them all again, the night a clatter of loose change
and every coin covers a date, spending the past away.
Every coin icy and ready to hold our eyelids down,
every coin says I'm part of a jackpot family, every
coin puts our trust in God but settles for cold cash
and a receipt.

The house moves through this sea.
Memories are spent money and our past is scattered
everywhere in a million tills and pockets, lost in the slots
of machines, flipped down bottomless wishing wells —
but now we travel over all these reminted coins, the house
going so fast we're standing still until we sleep.

In dreams we move on wheels, our old crackpot roadster
printing money as it goes, cat's paw tires making
counterfeits too true to be believed and our journey
back is over this landscape of money — all the coins
gone out of circulation, silver dollar and Buffalo nickel,
Indian head penny. Our tires punch them out like cookies.
The landscape of money blooms, coins turning red and blue
like poker chips that stack themselves in crazy mesas.
It is that dream
                of the nasal sound of cash the summer
people brought when they bought the lake in June,
the dream we never talked about though it burned all
winter like a low fever, the dream of Chris Craft
and Evinrude. Those boats cut furrows in the lake
but their owners never saw below their wakes nor could
they know what we knew was there — doom and ecstasy,
ghosts of friends, our wide-eyed monster; nor could
they ever know how winter snapped all that tremble
shut with ice and how the lake stayed that way
until the winning bet broke it up in spring;
now how we hated as we smiled their fever money
across our counters all summer.

Now those summer people sleep around us, wearing
their winter skins, making reservations for sand and water
in their dreams, polishing their boats edible, gritting
their teeth in sleep to keep their cabins whole
until July. We're all like bears sleeping through our
winter hours and sighing as our skin goes pale, losing
its dark memory of August, strangers to everything beyond
our double locks. With dog ears we hear the hibernating
whimpers, the nightmare wars all along the street
and we long too for the old lake, the place not called
home that is home, the place our wooden nickels take us,
the place so spent it's disappeared.

Some nights you travel back taking the whole
house, snail that you are, house-proud as you are,
calling it the big backpack, and you rumble over
money landscapes, scattering that gravel of nickels and dimes
wildly, the souped-up house spitting that crazy gravel.
But other nights, alone, you must crawl from one parking
meter to another buying back the past a half an hour
at a time, nickel and dimed to the poverty of nothingness.

XXI

Low Point

So, Low Point, we're there, energy
weak, bottles empty. It's
natural, it comes around —
you win on red but black
is always waiting.
                    Still we need
to take a chance on those old
slot machines, the silver dollars,
green cardtables under cones
of light. Getting there is always
a gamble wherever it is
so why not hit the joints again,
hear the banjos and the drums,
hear the tears of Saturday night
and rake in the chips.
                    Now we
move through the seven bars,
spot Slim on the fringe
of a good one, still steady but
beginning to list and preach
into the first room of his
drunk.
        Music lifts the roof
and the one-armed bandits
have mouths full of silver,
eyes of mixed fruit.
                    That's how
the weekends went, that
and dancing themselves to grease

trying to pound something more
from time,
            something more than
snow and tattered paychecks.
They wanted nights easy as dreams
but with a real taste, a real touch
so you felt it on your skin.
They wanted the secret flavor,
the final taste of days and nights
but mostly they got drunk
in the outskirts of what they sought,
the outskirts or even farther out,
alone on the prairies.
                But they
tried to make those bad nights flash
deep as a hidden mountain pool —
as we try —
            We need to break
through rock, break open the rock's
clenched hysteria, break into
that town they were after, the final
town, the town that was meant
to be.
        Of course we're sidetracked
as they were but we go on travelling,
go on looking for the right trail, the one
that finally leads straight
to the ancient town just over the next
hill, the town inside the rock.

XXII

The Impossible Light

We want the hard light of the dark,
the light struck from nothingness
and need, the light where no light is,
the impossible light of dead bulbs.
And so we move beyond water,
beyond trees, the great owl of the dark
toward some grainy piece of what
was lost, that diamond of gristle.

Tonight the trip is farther back.
I dig ancient loam and find rusty
cans and The Sweet Singer of Michigan.
But the drive is deeper than irony.
I dig my loam and yours as foxfire
stumps dream forges, mills burgeon
in grave mounds and we reach
a clearing in the woods, some hobo

jungle —
          I meet my father there
and our hands freeze together
on boxcar rungs through the Blue
Mountains. Of course we want the lost,
the lost so near, surrounding us
like an extra atmosphere, like that icy
air we breathed in the mountains,

our knuckles frozen to those rungs
waiting for summer.
                    Now I pick my way
walking high grass, then forest,

then the swamp
                    with its usual treachery.
The dark bleaches slowly
                    to summer light,

the rungs release my hands
and everything is almost there.
I breathe softly until
                    it grows its
third dimension
                    turning from paper
to its old solidity,
the summer we

dreamed
                    fastened to that boxcar.
But here it must be nursed
with caution
                    a kind of foreplay
within a dream.
                    Everything is still
the shadow-work of memory pumping
itself to roundness. Meadow
and swamp emerge. The sun plants
itself and invents the rest.
                    Meaning
sparks like downed wires —
                    some ropey force
spun from fibers too fine to braid,

some link giving a form that crumbles

as I touch its edge.
                    All this midnight
travel, this journey from winter,
leads to the shapeless shape, the salad
of meanings, this pick-up-sticks voyage
arrives at this wide place in the road,
this woods, this lake

                              and a summer day
we say frog and snake
                        joined
at the snake's mouth.
Our knuckles thaw
                    and we climb down
from that boxcar. For such

journeys every map is completely
white — with ice or vacancy —
and folded in that intricate way
but without a single mark.
We must invent terrain and route,
ink our fuel, chair and table
our pioneer utensils,
                        our conestoga biplane.

With them I meet the swampy
summer, melt winter from my
fingers, see snake and frog transformed
ready for their place on my flag.

XXIII

The Round Table

I go back to the round table,
spinning its perimeter, swimming
its familiar grain and feel
the end coming on, destination
preparing itself like a dinner,
like a kink in the road.
But zero falls and falls, the past
torn to this confetti, this frozen
dust of bones falling. With the snow
a maze descends, the map again
its old labyrinth invention,
syntax turned rubbery and loose,
aging, sentence and phrase
arthritic with remorse and ice,
our used-up language fallen to coma.
But enough of diagnosis!
Wake up the language! Without
words we lose the way for good.
Warm it ready by the old
heater. Let it get up with Slim
and bang in the black stove
with kindling. Let it boil thick
and bitter as the coffee he
thawed his bones with and turned
his brittle hands soft enough
to break six eggs in that inch
of bacon grease. We need words
at least as tough as those
rubber eggs freckled with pepper.

And so in the heart of winter
I thaw the words this way,
thaw until winter edges toward
spring and ice escapes my
marrow-ink and it flows
finding its way to the door
and out for a night of travel
toward those ancient summers
and the powdery earth of July,
the talcum of dust, all the ground
bones of all the royal animals.
And once again the earth is dusty
by the mill, earth ground to this
nothingness by the crusher
at Cascade Road & Gravel.
Now I see the dirt by the depot
where the ground cleared first
in spring. I finger the dust
and speak at last for everything lost.

XXIV

So Be It

Old poem
You preach
And the tree across the street
Is gone
      shaved smooth
Its stump like a huge wooden nickel

It omens the end
Journeys over
        the peace beyond the poem

And so the long poem
Of travel without arrival
Travels itself out like a typewriter ribbon
Feeding back and forth
Beginnings and endings blur

Without words we lose the way

Nameless all the lights go out

The old lake breaks up
Spring descends
On this round table

I wash my hands in that cold water
I stir the monster up
We stay alive with words

The poem of travel without arrival
Arrives

And some day when it's too late
To be too late
We'll found a town
And call it Smithereens

Vern Rutsala lives in Portland, Oregon, where he is professor of English at Lewis and Clark College. His earlier collections include *The Window, Laments, The Journey Begins, Paragraphs,* and *Walking Home from the Icehouse.* Awards for his work include a Guggenheim Fellowship and two fellowships from the National Endowment for the Arts.